SCIENCE CORNER

Day and Night

Alice Harman

WAYLAND

Explore the world with **Popcorn** - your complete first non-fiction library.

Look out for more titles in the Popcorn range. All books have the same format of simple text and striking images. Text is carefully matched to the pictures to help readers to identify and understand key vocabulary.
www.waylandbooks.co.uk/popcorn

Published in paperback in 2014 by Wayland
Copyright © Wayland 2014

Wayland
Hachette Children's Books
338 Euston Road
London NW1 3BH

Wayland Australia
Level 17/207 Kent Street
Sydney NSW 2000

 Produced for Wayland by
White-Thomson Publishing Ltd
www.wtpub.co.uk
+44 (0)843 208 7460

Editor: Alice Harman
Designer: Clare Nicholas
Picture researcher: Alice Harman
Series consultant: Kate Ruttle
Design concept: Paul Cherrill

British Library Cataloguing in Publication Data
Harman, Alice.
    Day and night. -- (Science corner)(Popcorn)
    1. Day--Juvenile literature. 2. Night--Juvenile
    literature.
    I. Title II. Series
    529.1-dc23

    ISBN: 978 0 7502 8315 1

Wayland is a division of Hachette Children's Books,
an Hachette UK company.
www.hachette.co.uk

Printed and bound in China

10 9 8 7 6 5 4 3 2 1

Picture/illustration credits:
Peter Bull 23; Stefan Chabluk 6; Dreamstime: Banol2007
13; Shutterstock: Anatoliy Samara 4, Zurijeta 5, SergiyN
7, solarseven 8, gravity imaging 10, Rob Wilson 10
inset, Konstantin Sutyagin 11, Stuart Monk 11 inset,
Sergios 12, Triff 14, Yarygin 14 inset, Triff 15, Lisa F. Young
16, Alexander Ishchenko 17, David Steele 18, Matej
Hudovernik 19, igor.steveanovic 20, formiktopus 21,
Pavelk cover; WTPix 9.

Every effort has been made to clear copyright.
Should there be any inadvertent omission,
please apply to the publisher for rectification.

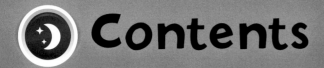 Contents

What are day and night?   4

Light and darkness   6

Sunrise and sunset   8

Around the world   10

Shadows   12

Moon and stars   14

Temperature   16

Animals   18

Plants   20

Day or night?   22

Make a sundial   23

Glossary   24

Index   24

What are day and night?

In the day, it is light outside.
The Sun gives out this light.
The Sun is a star, and the
Earth circles around it.

Do not look at the Sun. Its light is very strong and it can badly hurt your eyes.

On sunny days, the light from the Sun is very bright.

At night, it is dark outside. Most
people sleep through the night
and wake up the next morning.

We use electric lights, such as
bedside lamps, to see when it is dark.

Light and darkness

The Earth spins as it goes around the Sun. The Sun shines on the part of the Earth that faces it.

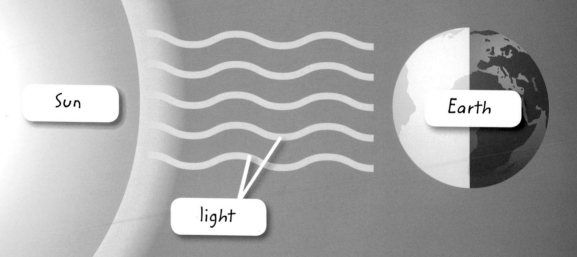

Sun

light

Earth

When the Sun shines on one area of the Earth, it is day there.

The Sun cannot shine on the part of the Earth's surface that is turned away from it. When there is no light from the Sun, it is dark.

The Earth is always turning, but we can't feel it move.

When an area of the Earth is turned away from the Sun, it is night there.

Sunrise and sunset

We see more and more of the Sun as the Earth turns towards it. The Sun seems to rise in the sky, but it doesn't move. It is the Earth that is moving.

Sunrise is the time in the morning when the Sun first appears.

It doesn't go straight from day
to night. As the Earth turns away
from the Sun, it slowly gets darker.

Sunset is the
time when
the Sun seems
to get lower
and lower in
the sky.

Around the world

When it is light on one side of the Earth, it is dark on the opposite side. When it is day in the United Kingdom, it is night in Australia.

The Sydney Opera House in Australia is lit up with electric lights at night.

Sydney Opera House

The London Eye in the United Kingdom

Two sides of a big country can be
quite far apart on the Earth's surface.
One area can be turned towards the
Sun before the rest of the country.

In the USA, when it is sunset in Los Angeles in the
west, it is already dark in New York in the east.

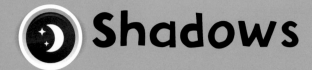 Shadows

When the Sun shines on an object, there are areas of darkness behind the object where the Sun can't shine. These are called shadows.

Any objects that aren't see-through can have a shadow.

Some days are less bright than others because sometimes clouds get in front of the Sun. These clouds block the Sun and create shadows on the Earth below.

It is light above the clouds, but the Earth underneath is in the clouds' shadow.

Moon and stars

The Moon circles around the Earth. One side of the Moon is bright because it reflects light from the Sun. The other side is dark because it is in shadow.

Sometimes we see all of the bright side of the Moon. When some of its dark side is turned towards us, it appears as a thinner shape.

The Moon does not give out its own light.

The Sun and all other stars give out light. Other stars you can see in the sky are not as bright as the Sun. This is because they are much further away.

In the countryside, you can often see lots of stars. In the city, the bright electric lights make it difficult to see the stars at night.

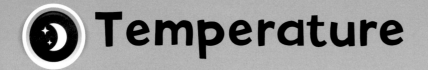 Temperature

The Sun gives out heat as well as light. It is warmer during the day, when our part of the Earth faces the Sun.

On a sunny day, you can feel that it is cooler when you sit in a dark shadow.

The Earth takes in the heat from the Sun, and warms up during the day. It loses this heat bit by bit at night.

Thick jumpers and a campfire help to keep people warm when they camp outside at night.

 Animals

Many animals, including humans, like to move around during the day and sleep at night.

Camels have short, thick fur to protect their skin from the heat and light of the Sun.

Nocturnal animals, such as the tarsier, like to sleep through the day and look for food at night.

Nocturnal animals often have very big eyes that help them to see well in the dark.

Each of the tarsier's eyes is as big as its brain!

 Plants

Most plants need light from
the Sun. They use it for energy.
It keeps them alive and helps
them grow.

Plants take in sunlight through their leaves.

Some plants slowly turn to face the Sun through the day. This helps them get as much light as possible.

Sunflowers can grow very tall if they take in lots of light.

The tallest ever sunflower was taller than three grown men standing on top of each other!

Day or night?

Read through the sentences below. Some of them describe things that happen in the day, and others describe what happens at night. Try to work out whether each sentence is talking about day or night.

1. It is dark unless we use electric lights.

2. Plants take in light from the Sun.

3. Nocturnal animals move around and look for food.

4. The Sun warms up the Earth.

5. Shadows appear behind objects.

6. The Moon and stars appear bright in the sky.

7. Our part of the Earth is turned away from the Sun.

8. People go to sleep in their beds.

Make a sundial

Before people had clocks, they used sundials to tell the time. The place of the shadow on the sundial shows how far our part of the Earth is turned towards the Sun.

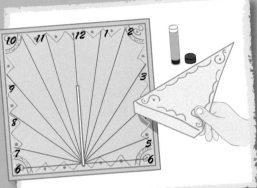

1. Stick each printed template onto a piece of card, and cut them both out. Ask an adult to cut a slit along the dotted line on the square template. Decorate the square with different colours and patterns.

2. Decorate the triangle. Fold over the tab on the bottom of the triangle along the dotted line.

3. Put the tab through the slit in the square, and stick it down to the other side of the square. Make sure that the triangle points towards the number 12 on the square.

4. Ask an adult to help you find north using the compass. Then place your sundial on a flat surface, with the arrow pointing the same way as the compass. If it's sunny, you can tell the time! (In summer time, add an hour to the time that your sundial shows.)

Visit our website to download the printable templates for this project.

www.waylandbooks.co.uk/popcorn

Glossary

block get in the way of something

camp sleep in a tent that is set up outside

east one of the four main points of direction that people use to measure where something is on Earth; east is directly opposite west

electric describes something that uses electricity to work

fur hair that covers the bodies of some animals

reflect when a surface throws back something in a different direction

star large, round object far away in space; stars give off light and heat; the Sun is the closest star to Earth

west one of the four main points of direction that people use to measure where something is on Earth; west is directly opposite east

Index

animals 18–19

clouds 13

dark 5, 7, 9, 10, 11, 12, 14, 19

day 4, 6, 9, 13, 16, 17, 18, 19

Earth 4, 6, 7, 8, 9, 10, 11, 13, 14, 16, 17

east 11

electric lights 5, 10, 15

heat 16, 17

light 4, 7, 10, 13, 14, 15, 16, 20, 21

Moon 14

night 5, 7, 9, 10, 15, 17, 18, 19

plants 20–21

shadow 12, 13, 14, 16

sky 8, 15

sleep 5, 19

star 4, 15

Sun 4, 6, 7, 8, 9, 11, 12, 13, 14, 15, 16, 17, 18, 20, 21

sunrise 8

sunset 9

temperature 16–17

west 11

Popcorn

SCIENCE CORNER
Day and Night

Discover what makes day light and night dark, and how important this is in everyday life.

- See why it is day in the UK when it is night in Australia.

- Learn about the Sun, the Moon and the stars you see at night.

- Find out what shadows are, and what causes them.

Alice Harman is a writer and editor specialising in children's educational publishing.

The consultant, Kate Ruttle, is a freelance literacy consultant providing INSET and school support, particularly in East Anglia. She is currently the Literacy Co-ordinator, Special Needs Co-ordinator, and Deputy Headteacher at a primary school in Suffolk.

Titles in the series

978-0-7502-8304-5

978-0-7502-8315-1

978-0-7502-8316-8

978-0-7502-8317-5

978-0-7502-8318-2

For free downloadable resources, go to www.waylandbooks.co.uk/popcorn

28749

WAYLAND
www.waylandbooks.co.uk

£7.99

ISBN 978-0-7502-8315-1

9 780750 283151

KR-708-787